The Clothes they Wore
17th and 18th Centuries

by Nellie Roberts

illustrated by Helen Herbert

Cambridge University Press

Cambridge
New York   New Rochelle
Melbourne   Sydney

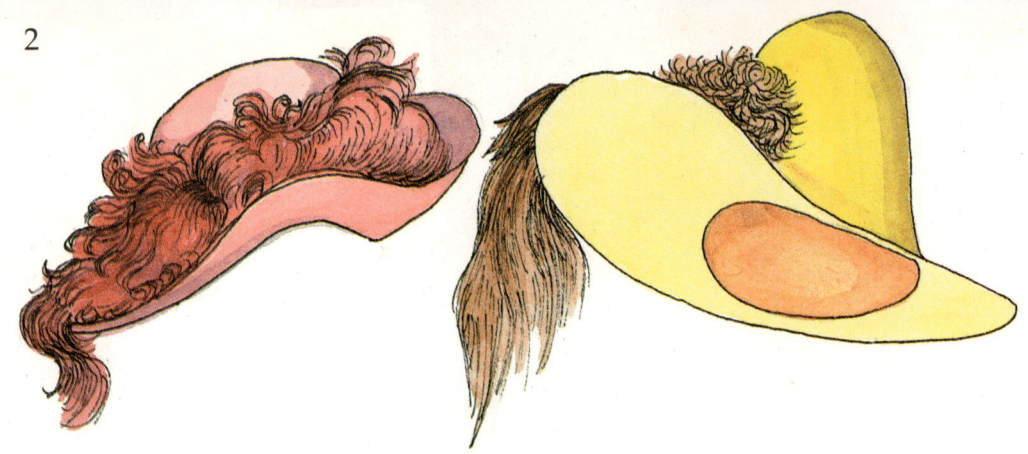

CHANGING FASHION Clothes changed a lot between the years 1600 and 1800. At the beginning of the period people were still affected by the idea that people in the reign of Queen Elizabeth I had that clothes and jewellery reflected a person's importance. Gradually flashy, extravagant fashions gave way to elegance, then to the severe clothes of the time of Oliver Cromwell, the 1650's. The rather tasteless clothes covered with trimmings of the early years of Charles II's reign, the 1660's, were a reaction against this. Then dress became plainer, although the materials were still very rich. Coats and waistcoats were embroidered, knee breeches and silk stockings were worn, lace foamed at the necks and wrists of shirts, and of ladies' dresses. Hair was covered by wigs, at first big and curly, then smaller and powdered. At first they were worn just by men, later by everybody. Ladies' styles altered greatly through the 17th and 18th centuries; dresses, sometimes with the fullness at the sides, sometimes at the back, were

stiff or softly gathered; hair was dressed in ringlets or in formal powdered arrangements. Country people, depending on whether they could afford it, wore tougher and harder-wearing copies of the fashion of the day. For the poorest people, rags and tatters were, as always, the order of the day.

During the last twenty years or so of the 18th century, wealthy people began to wear clothes meant for use and not just for show. A change had been slowly going on for some years, but the French Revolution and the disappearance of the French court made their fussy, extravagant way of dressing unpopular. This book shows some of the changes in style during the 17th and 18th centuries, a period of extremes, ranging in fashion from showy extravagance to sober plainness, and a period in which people went through wars and revolutions.

THE AGE OF PROSPERITY Queen Elizabeth I, who died in 1603, had always been a leader of fashion, and the ladies of her court copied her clothes. Not so with her successors, James I and his wife, the Danish princess who became Queen Anne. King James, except for having his suits padded because he was afraid of being stabbed, was not interested in clothes and was not even very clean or tidy.

Queen Anne wore the formal styles of Queen Elizabeth's day. But as there were many splendid gowns left in the old Queen's wardrobe, it may be that Anne just wanted to make use of them. Elizabeth had often passed on clothes when she had finished with them and Anne liked dressing up and taking part in musical plays with her ladies. Once they dressed as negresses, another time as sea goddesses, but whatever the costume Anne always insisted that her hoop, or farthingale, that made her dresses stand out around her, must form part of the costume. This farthingale was a wire cage shaped like a drum, which fastened round the waist. It made the skirt stand out straight from the waist for about eighteen inches and then fall vertically to the floor.

During James's reign, men wore baggy breeches attached to their doublets, or jackets, by metal tags and covered over by belts or sashes. Doublets were tight-fitting, with whalebone panels at the waist like corsets. Ruffs, heavily starched and uncomfortable around the neck, gave way to 'falling' collars with the neckband of the collar tucked inside the doublet and the collar 'falling' outside. Stockings of silk or fine wool were held up by garters. Elastic had not been invented, so the garters were simply strips of woven or knitted material, tied round the leg. Boots of soft leather reached above the knee when pulled up but were often turned over at the top like modern ladies' boots. Shoes were decorated with rosettes, with red painted heels for grand occasions. Cloaks were worn out of doors, with tall round-topped 'sugar loaf' hats, so called because sugar was made into blocks, or 'loaves', using moulds of the same shape.

Clothes in the country had to be hard-wearing and practical, so styles changed more slowly. Countrymen wore long thigh-boots, and jerkins or tunics of leather over their doublets. Their wives did not wear the hoops which supported the skirts of fashionable ladies, as these were cumbersome and worn only for show. These simple styles were encouraged by various laws (called 'Sumptuary Laws') passed in an attempt to prevent ordinary people imitating the upper classes. However nobody seems to have taken much notice of these laws.

AN AGE OF LACE When Charles I came to the throne in 1625, he and his wife Henrietta Maria created a new look in clothes. This was partly due to the new Queen's French style, as well as the influence of Charles's friends such as the artists Peter Paul Rubens and Anthony van Dyck. Breeches became longer reaching down to below the knee, and were less baggy. Doublets fitted less tightly, soft boots were popular, and hats became wider brimmed and decorated with ostrich plumes. Men grew their hair longer and small, pointed beards and moustaches came into fashion. There were lace trimmings everywhere, on the edges of collars, cuffs and even boot-tops. Ladies wore filmy collars of lace. Most lace came from such towns as Valenciennes in France, and Brussels and Mechlin in Flanders, famous centres of lacemaking. No machines had yet been invented to make lace so it was all made by hand and was very expensive.

Anyone wearing a great deal of lace was instantly recognised as wealthy and important.

The King's artist friend, van Dyck, painted many portraits of men and women at Charles's court wearing this beautiful lace, and the huge lace collars of the time are called van Dyck collars to this day. He also painted courtiers with the fashionable small pointed beards and moustaches of the time and these became known as van Dyck beards.

Queen Henrietta Maria introduced new styles for ladies. Farthingales disappeared, skirts were long and full, while hair hung in ringlets and was often threaded with pearls. Ladies wore beautiful 'falling' or 'standing' collars of lace, and wide hats with plumes of feathers. The waists of their dresses moved higher and often had a short, split over-skirt. The sleeves of their dresses were covered with ribbons, or slashed showing the silk beneath.

PLAIN AND PURITAN With Charles I as an example, his courtiers had always been encouraged to dress and behave well. But the kingdom was crumbling under his rule; he could not agree with his Parliament and a bloody Civil War broke out. His opponents, named Puritans, have been called 'right but repulsive'! Quite reasonably, they objected to Charles insisting on running the country single-handed. Unfortunately, they also thought that everyone should be as stern and serious as themselves.

Even during the Civil War, 1642–49, Charles's Cavaliers wore feathered hats, jackets and breeches with fancy trimmings. They had large moustaches and wore their hair long and curled. Their swords hung from embroidered shoulder-belts.

Oliver Cromwell the Puritan general, put his soldiers into a very different style of dress – plain, hardwearing clothes with iron helmets and breastplates. Because their hair was usually cropped short they were called Roundheads. Their battle dress was the most practical worn until the 20th century. Civilian Puritans wore dark suits and tall black hats. Puritan ladies wore grey dresses and neat white caps. Those who disliked completely plain clothes got around the ban on frivolity by embroidering them with texts from the Bible!

Cromwell defeated the King, took over the Government and made severe laws. But one thing he learned he could not do was to force everyone to dress alike! After the war enough people had money to spend to bring fashion alive again. Non-Puritans dressed in fine clothes copied from French styles. One favourite for men was a short jacket, like a bolero with sleeves, worn with short, wide 'petticoat' breeches, like a divided skirt. Samuel Pepys, who wrote his famous diary at this time, mentions buying a *jackanapes* jacket, meaning one of these short garments. This expression has come down to us in the jackets worn at Eton College and called 'monkey jackets' – jackanapes being an old word for monkey. Jackets, breeches, hats and shoes were all heavily trimmed with ribbons wherever these could be attached.

A Puritan family

THE RETURN OF GAIETY   After eleven years in power, Cromwell died. King Charles II, the son of Charles I, came back from France, where he had been in exile. At once he cancelled Cromwell's laws against theatres and all other amusements – even Christmas parties! Among other things, people were once more allowed to dance around a maypole on May Day.

Charles must have looked something like a maypole himself – 6 feet 6 inches (2 metres) tall and wearing magnificent clothes covered with ribbons. For many years he and his friends had been living in poverty abroad and it was no wonder that they now revelled in their fine houses and gorgeous dress.

Luckily, Charles had 'style', which meant he knew what looked right and what did not. After a while he saw that these gaudy clothes, covered with fussy trimmings, were out of place. He took up a new fashion, said to be inspired by the clothes of the East, although to our eyes it does not look it. It consisted of neat, dark breeches, fastened with a band just below the knee, a 'vest', like a waistcoat with sleeves, and a long jacket just covering the knees. At first the jacket was quite loose, fastening with a few buttons at the bottom, but later it became tight-waisted. When Charles first appeared in this style his courtiers bet him that it would not catch on, but, because it could be worn by almost anybody, it became very popular. In London at least, even quite ordinary people dressed as grandly as they could and noblemen made up the same style in brocades and velvets and satin. Samuel Pepys who was a civil servant, as well as a diarist, had a best suit of purple velvet trimmed with gold lace. But he also had some badly fitting shoes, and the first time he went out in his new suit, had to hobble home with a blistered heel! In the country, farmers and innkeepers wore the same style of suit in tougher materials, like buckskin, very soft, well tanned and hard-wearing leather, or fine, woollen broadcloth.

petticoat breeches

SPLENDOUR AND DIRT

It was during the reign of Charles II that men began wearing wigs. Advertisements asked people to sell their hair, if it was long and nicely coloured. Although the price of these wigs was enormous, the fashion became so popular that everyone who could afford it, and some who could not, had at least one. Thieves even trained little boys to sit on their shoulders and snatch wigs from the heads of their owners as they walked by in the street.

Ladies too now began to wear gayer clothes. Long-waisted dresses were fashionable again, laced tightly over stiff corsets although dresses worn loose and flowing – 'undress' – were also popular. The dresses themselves were of silk or satin, sometimes caught up at the side to show a lace-trimmed petticoat. Coloured silk stockings and high-heeled shoes were worn and fashionable women dressed their hair in ringlets, tied with coloured ribbons or pearls. They also began to make up their faces again.

Ladies who were not so rich imitated Court fashions, including the use of make-up. It was not really attractive, because face powder was a chalky white, like talcum powder, and, what was worse, it contained lead. We know now that lead is dangerous and poisonous, but they did not. Although the powder helped to whiten the skin, the lead in it caused many spots and pimples. Many people also had scars from skin diseases such as smallpox. These blemishes were covered with 'patches' – little designs cut out in black sticky paper.

Although ladies made up heavily, they rarely thought to wash their faces or bodies. In fact no-one was particularly clean. People did not realise the connection between cleanliness and health and saw no reason to bathe very often. In fact they thought that baths were unhealthy.

The same applied to washing clothes. Linen underclothes were made from a tough fibre called flax, which washes well. But outer clothes were made mainly of woollen cloth or a wool mixture, and too much rubbing and scrubbing causes wool fibres to mat and become stiff and scratchy. Silk, satin or velvet would spoil in the wash. Because of this, outer clothes were seldom washed.

When their clothes looked too dirty, wealthy people passed them on to their servants, who either sold them or wore them themselves. Sometimes, especially grand clothes were passed on to companies of actors at one of the theatres. Infectious diseases were often passed on by people who had suffered from them giving away their clothes without having them cleaned.

WILLIAM AND MARY: THE RISE OF THE COTTON TRADE

After the death of Charles II in 1685, his brother James became King. But there was a threatened rebellion and James II fled to France, leaving his daughter Mary and her husband William, who was ruler of Holland, to take over. William III was not very interested in how he looked and had no influence on fashion, which changed little for a number of years. Men's coats did become gradually tighter and fuller skirted, with pleats at the sides and huge turnback cuffs, and these were worn over longer waistcoats and tighter-fitting breeches. Square-toed shoes were common, but for riding boots were worn, or sometimes gaiters over shoes. Men still wore big curly wigs and wide-brimmed hats decorated with braid, lace or feathers.

The most noticeable thing about ladies' dress at this time was a new head-dress called a *fontange*. It was copied from the invention of a French lady of that name, and made up of several frills of lace and linen pleated over a wire frame, with the ends hanging over the shoulders. Lace was worn a great deal and was very valuable. Since it could be packed up small and easily hidden it was often smuggled from France and Holland. For similar reasons it was a popular thing to steal, though the punishment was heavy – if caught, people were 'transported' to America and made to stay there for the rest of their lives.

Towards the end of the 17th century the north of England became the centre of the cloth trade. The people of Yorkshire had been keeping sheep and making woollen cloth for a long time, and now cotton was being woven in the neighbouring county, Lancashire. The raw cotton was brought from the Middle East and India by ship to London, taken by pack-horse to Manchester and given out to people who worked at home, spinning the cotton on spinning wheels, and weaving it on hand looms. Many places in the north still have 'weavers houses' where the top floor is one large room, with big windows letting in plenty of light. Here the hand looms were set up.

Everyone liked cotton, because it was light, easy to wash and could be dyed and printed in attractive colours. Bed covers and curtains, as well as clothes, were made from the new material.

MILITARY STYLES During the reign of Mary's sister Anne, England was at war with France. There was a warlike feeling in the air, with popular songs and jokes about recruiting sergeants who tried to persuade young men to join the army. At this time the modern style of army was founded and regiments were formed that still exist today. Some regiments still wear copies of the original uniforms, so we can get an idea of how soldiers looked in the early eighteenth century. Heavy wigs were not suitable for army life so soldiers wore a lighter type with a long plait at the back. Soon other men began to follow the soldiers' example.

Coats and waistcoats for civilians, however, were still very grand, with wonderful embroidery. As with lacemaking, all embroidery was done by hand, and making garments took a lot of effort. Embroiderers were employed as what is now called 'sweated labour'. They worked extremely hard for very long hours and got very little money. Sadly, many workers ruined their eyesight by peering at the fine stitchery. Their workrooms were rough, cold places, very different from the grand houses in which the beautiful garments they made were worn.

A ladies' fashion called the *sack* appeared during Queen Anne's reign. This was an overdress with a loose back panel falling into a small train, its elbow-length sleeves had frills of lace. The *fontange* headdress gave way to a little cap with streamers, and ladies wore fancy aprons.

At this time, few streets were paved, and they were often a mass of churned up mud. So a style worn by peasants since the middle ages – wooden clogs, called pattens – was now worn by ladies over their shoes to protect them and lift them out of the dirt. Pattens had a thick wooden sole, and uppers to match the shoe.

THE FRENCH INFLUENCE When Queen Anne died in 1714, a distant cousin, who was the ruler of a small district of Germany called Hanover, became King of England as George I. He was always thought of as a foreigner, could not speak English when he arrived and never learnt it properly. He influenced British life very little, least of all in dress.

Perhaps because of this, French fashion had a lot of influence in Britain. The French court was the richest and most splendid in Europe, and everyone else copied what was worn there. English noblemen at court wore silks and satins, powdered wigs and lace cravats just like the courtiers of Paris. But, outside the court, even the wealthy men began to prefer fine woollen suits without so much trimming. Of course, country folk still dressed more simply and were influenced only gradually by new styles, although they liked to look as smart as they could. Men continued to wear wigs, although these were smaller and had the ends tied at the back of the neck in a velvet bow.

From paintings of the time, it seems that all wealthy men were stout, for whether or not they took exercise, they ate and drank a great deal. Their style of dress changed little for a long time, though a heavy overcoat with capes came to be worn for cold weather. It was called a greatcoat and was made of thick woollen material.

Our idea about how highwaymen dressed comes from this time – a thick greatcoat to keep him warm while waiting on his horse for a coach to pass, a cocked hat, riding boots, a mask and of course a pistol or two, were almost a uniform. Heavy coaches trundled about the country roads – easy prey for a man on a fast horse, and there was a lot of this sort of crime. It was partly because there was no well organised group like our police force to enforce law and order, and partly because there were many very poor people who either thieved or starved, especially those living in big towns.

HOOPS By the middle of the 18th century ladies' fashions had developed very oddly, with full skirts draped over hooped petticoats and spreading out at the sides. The wearers looked rather as though they were wearing sofas, and it was necessary for them to move sideways like crabs along passages or narrow places. When two ladies met in a corridor, one would have to reverse to somewhere wider, before they could pass. Then someone cleverly thought of hingeing each side of the hoop, so that it could be lifted up.

The dresses were low-necked and long-waisted. They were worn, as earlier, over stiff corsets. A lady at the court of Louis XV in France, called the Marquise de Pompadour, started a style of decorative trimming called ruching, which was gathered lengths of satin sewn on to her dresses. With this trimming, ribbons and artificial flowers were worn, with a velvet ribbon around the neck.

Fans were used a great deal, and there was a whole language of signs which could be made by using a fan. Well-bred girls were not supposed to speak to men they didn't know, so fans were often very useful! These same ladies continued to use chalky face powder, and to rouge their lips and cheeks, and powder their hair.

Working girls had a style of dress of their own during the 1700's. They wore striped or flower-patterned cottons and chintzes, now woven in the new mills of Lancashire. Filmy muslin scarves, worn around their necks, came from India. Milkmaids wore striped petticoats with gay overskirts looped up at the sides, with laced bodices and buckled shoes.

In the year 1745, there was an unsuccessful rebellion, led by Charles Edward Stuart, the grandson of James II, who had been forced off the throne. Charles Stuart was popularly known as Bonny Prince Charlie and was supported mainly in Scotland. His Highland army was defeated at the battle of Culloden in 1746, and the government punished the few survivors very severely. Amongst other penalties Scotsmen were forbidden to wear Highland dress, especially the tartan kilt, and had to wear dull-coloured trousers instead. In 1782 the ban was lifted and at once they went back to wearing the clan tartans of which Highlanders were, and are, very proud. Ironically, the style of Highland dress now worn by civilians and soldiers alike is actually a military style.

MACARONIS AND JACK TARS

All this time men were still wearing wigs. Dandies or 'Macaronis', so called because they had visited Italy and thought everything Italian was smart, wore wigs dressed into a point at the top of their heads. They were the people meant in the song of the time:

> 'Yankie Doodle came to London
> On a yellow pony
> Put a feather in his cap
> And called it Macaroni.'

The War of Independence was being fought between the Americans (Yankees) and the British who liked to make fun of them.

A smart Macaroni wore a jacket which, although still quite long, was cut away at the front to allow the wearer to stride freely. It was usually made of woollen material, with a high turndown collar, often of velvet. For very grand wear the coat was made of embroidered silk or velvet. For ordinary wear fine cloth, untrimmed, was worn. Fancy waistcoats appeared, worn with evening clothes. Quite short waistcoats, which were double-breasted and often striped, went with plain day suits. Macaronis, just to be different, wore striped breeches.

Working men had been wearing braces for a long time, but now smart people adopted this sensible fashion. Breeches, like coats, became tighter fitting, made of heavy cloth or buckskin, which looked well and was hard wearing.

A few years before the American War of Independence started, the British navy was put into an official uniform designed in the fashion of the day. There had been some argument about what colours the sailors should wear. The story goes that the King happened to see the pretty Duchess of Bedford wearing a dark blue and white riding habit in the park. He was so struck that he insisted that the Navy should wear the same colours. So 'navy' coats and white breeches, 'navy' cocked hats with gold braid, and white knee stockings, became the rule for officers. 'Ratings', ordinary sailors, wore loose white pantaloons and flat-crowned, round-brimmed hats. Their longish hair was plaited into a tight little pigtail, which was tarred. Because of this the name Jack Tar for a sailor became popular

woman and child 1779

SCULPTURED HAIR Fashions still followed the French court, where Marie Antoinette, the Queen, started a fad for dressing up in a make-believe version of a shepherdess costume – just like Bo-peep – when she went to amuse herself at her model farm, which had a very small collection of clean animals. The sheep were washed and trimmed with bows, and housed in clean little sheds for the Queen's amusement.

Later she had an even more quaint idea. This was wearing a towering arrangement of hair, brushed up from the face and piled over pads of wool and false hair, stiffened with grease and powdered heavily. On top of all this were added – flowers, feathers and even model ships! Surprisingly the fashion caught on. When the War of Independence was being fought, a cartoon showed the Battle of Bunker Hill taking place on the summit of someone's hair-do! There were tiny cannons and tents arranged on opposing hillocks of hair. If he had thought of it, the cartoonist could have added mice in little cocked hats firing the cannon. These creatures, believe it or not, sometimes got into a lady's hair arrangement and settled down to eat the grease with which it was stiffened.

To cover these monstrous piles of hair, ladies wore huge boudoir caps of muslin, lace and ribbon, and outsize cavalier-type hats, top-heavy with feathers. If they wanted to travel by carriage they had to kneel on the floor to make room for their hair, and it was surprising that ladies could hold up their heads at all under such a load. Several ladies were burnt when their hair caught fire from the candles of hanging chandeliers as they passed beneath them. This fashion was really too extreme to last and there was soon a return to a soft, natural style. It must have been a great relief.

Powdering the hair was such a messy operation that in large houses a tiny room called a powder closet was set aside for the purpose. People wore capes over their clothes, and masks over their faces, while powder was applied to their hair. Wigs, of course, could be powdered before being put on.

JOHN BULL The second half of the eighteenth century produced great changes. The Americans won the War of Independence in 1783 and broke away from Britain. Their new Constitution, which proclaimed that all men were free and equal, impressed the French in particular, who were growing discontented with their extravagant rulers. There were threats of trouble long before the French Revolution broke out and the Court realised it would have to change its style to some extent. Aristocrats began to dress more quietly and imitated the riding clothes of the British upper classes. In Britain itself, the high heels and powdered wigs of the Macaronis and the huge headdresses and spreading skirts of the ladies also gave way to simpler styles.

Men's clothes did not change much, but they did become plainer. Once, it would have been easy to tell a nobleman from, say, a banker or wealthy businessman by his clothes, but now it was becoming difficult. They all wore well-fitting coats cut away from the waist at the front and split into two 'tails' at the back. The waistcoat had shrunk from being a real coat into a sleeveless, waist-length garment, just showing under the tail-coat.

About this time the figure of John Bull, invented some years earlier in a political pamphlet, began to be used to represent the typical Englishman. He wore tight-fitting, light-coloured breeches, a top hat, a tail coat and high boots. He was rather portly and red-faced, and looked like a well-to-do farmer. His large waistcoat showed the Union Jack flag.

But tight breeches were going out of fashion in favour of loose pantaloons, or trousers. Because of the change which took place in children's clothes in the middle of the eighteenth century, many younger men had worn them as children and knew they were warmer and more comfortable than breeches. These early trousers, though, were extra long and had straps which went under the soles of the shoes.

WHAT CHILDREN WORE Until about 1750, children, once they had passed the baby stage, were dressed like little grown-ups. Rich people were fond of having their family portraits painted and in galleries and museums you can see many pictures of these stiffly posed little folk – the small girls in tight-waisted dresses, the boys, like their fathers, in breeches, waistcoats and coats. Their families were extremely concerned with appearances and even the clothes of tiny children were made of unsuitable, heavy materials like brocade, velvet and satin, and were heavily trimmed. Little girls, sometimes only two or three years old, were stuffed into tight corsets. A painting of the time by Gainsborough shows four small children, all, even the youngest, a toddler, in these restricting clothes.

Little boys, until the age of about six, wore dresses. Paintings of the time often show a child with the face and expression of a little boy wearing a floor-length dress. But when a boy eventually reached 6 or 7 and was 'breeched' he was put into a stiff suit, becoming in a single day a little man.

Houses were usually cold and draughty. Mothers and nurses were more concerned with keeping infants warm than exercising their arms and legs, so they wrapped long woollen bandages round the infants, making them look like little mummies. Babies usually wore these 'swaddling clothes' until they were about six months old, and very unhealthy they must have been. Swaddling clothes were worn by babies until the early 1700's, when long dresses began to be used instead. To keep them warm, toddlers and little girls normally wore caps over their hair. When little ones did start to walk, they wore floor-length dresses, and were controlled by reins called 'leading-strings'. Probably to protect toddlers from the falls which must have resulted from tripping over their long dresses, they often wore a kind of 'skid-lid' around the head, made from a rolled pad of material. This was called a 'black pudding', because, if made of black material, it looked very much like the sausage of the same name. The painter Rubens sketched his baby son wearing one, and very quaint he looks, too.

Of course, changes in fashion did not stop at the end of the 18th century. You can read about the changing styles of clothes in the 19th and 20th centuries in the next book in this series.

1630 1640

1700 1710 1730 1740

PLACES TO VISIT

The Museum of Costume
Assembly Rooms
Bath

Cheltenham Art Gallery and Museum
Clarence Street
Cheltenham

Museum of Childhood
38 High Street
Edinburgh

Royal Scottish Museum
Chambers Street
Edinburgh

Art Gallery and Museum
Kelvingrove
Glasgow

Bethnal Green Museum of Childhood
Cambridge Heath Road
London

Victoria and Albert Museum
South Kensington
London

The Museum of London
London Wall
London

The Gallery of English Costume
Platt Hall
Rusholme
Manchester

Costume Galleries
Castle Howard
York

York Castle Museum
Tower Street
York